Dirty Talking & Texting Tips....!!

THIS IS A CARLTON BOOK

First published in 2011
Reprinted in 2014
by Carlton Books Limited
20 Mortimer Street
London W1T 3JW

10 9 8 7 6 5

Design and text copyright © Carlton Books Limited 2011

A CIP catalogue record for this book is available from the British Library.

ISBN 978 1 84732 411 5

Printed and bound in Italy

Dirty Talking & Texting Tips....!!

LISA SWEET

CARLTON BOOKS

CONTENTS

Introduction

Face it: we need all the tools we can get when it comes to catching someone's attention.

Texting (and its first cousin, the instant message) is rapidly becoming the easiest and most convenient way of courting, bonding and simply planning time together. Chances are, you have texted someone in the last five minutes.

Like a caramel latte, text offers near-instant gratification. No matter what you're doing, you can be connected mentally as well as literally. All it takes is the push and stroke of a few keys to reach out and touch that special someone, whether it's to just say "Hi!" or to get down and dirty and reveal your raunchiest fantasies. That's the magic of a text: you can be as bold as you dare!

So the question isn't whether getting it on digitally is OK, but rather, how do you do it? Instant love notes can be anything but simple. This book contains everything you need to know for improving your text life. The future of your relationship is in your hands, literally!

FLIRXTING

Texts are the new love notes. An email feels stiff and polite, like those thank you notes your mother used to make you write. Calling can make you look a little desperate. But a text? Sending an informal message via your mobile takes the angst out of hooking up with that tall, dark and handsome special someone. You can flirt, set up dates and even whisper – well, spell out – sweet nothings without the risk of a red face or stumbling over your reply. Since no message is sent until you hit "send", you can leisurely think and edit your message to your heart's content.

Plus, texts do the heavy lifting for you. With a few witty messages bantered back and forth, you can quickly stoke enough attraction that you won't have to do that much in-person flirting moves when you finally do get together.

As your relationship becomes more serious, a quick steamy text sent at lunchtime may be all you need to stay connected – and to get in the mood to physically connect later that day. Bottom line: relationships depend on communication, and texting is a lot faster and more convenient than email or a phone call for keeping in touch.

The Text Steps

Sexual tension can be rapidly ratcheted up with texting… but it can be just as quickly crashed. Think of it this way: if you met in person, you'd work some bodacious hair flips and eye gazes to lure him in. How can you electronically replace touching a man's knee, running your hands along his back, or any number of your signature come-hither moves, and be sure he won't "86" your message without even reading your missive? The words you use and the timing you choose count. The following is your unlimited flirxting plan with everything you need to take you from ";ing" at him to your first "ILY".

7 Rules of Thumb

DON'T PRESS "SEND" UNTIL YOU'VE READ THE FOLLOWING.

RULE 1

Don't over-text.

Unless you're having a back-and-forth conversation via SMS, your random, spur of the mo' texts shouldn't be clogging his inbox. It was cute to send him a smile at 8 pm and to follow-up with a wink at 8.10 pm, but a third emoticon at 8.15 pm gets annoying and another at 8.30 pm and he's going to think that you're a cyberstalker. If you don't know him, two texts within the space of an hour are acceptable – after that, back away from your handheld electronic device. If you've already been on a few dates, you can send him "Thinking of you" texts a maximum of three times in one day. He'll get the message.

Bad Connection: "Did u get my text?" Unless your text was intercepted by MI5 (and it wasn't), he got your message, loud and clear. If you want to poke him to respond, keep it jokey so you don't seem annoying: "My mother texts faster than u!"

2
RULE

Remember, he's a man.

This means two things: first, he probably won't (or know how to) respond to mundane messages like "Just wanted to say Hi!"; second, he likes to get to the point. Some guys will say that their phone is a communication tool, and therefore there are only three acceptable texts a person can send or receive: "I'm 18", "Where R U?" and "Do U want sex?" In other words, until you know him and his likes and communication abilities better, stick with relaying the information you want him to hear – even if that info is "I like you". Keep it light and simple.

"Hey, QT – wanna get
2gether 2night?"
"Good morning, handsome!"
(first thing in the morning)
"I'm in the mood for a kiss."

3
RULE

Don't use too many acronyms unless you know that he'll get your message.

You might write "ASL" as a quick way of asking him his age, if he's into girls and where he wants to meet up, and he thinks you're calling him an a**hole. Even if he only speaks in text, you still have to take care as some abbreviations double up – for instance, LOL could mean Laughing Out Loud or it may mean Lots of Love. ILY might mean I Love You or I Like You. So until you know his shorthand style, limit yourself to the following:

2 – to
R – are
U – you
yday – yesterday

11

4 RULE

Pick your tone.

It's impossible to read how a person is saying something in a text. Even a completely harmless message can be easily taken the wrong way – let alone some light sarcasm or a one-line joke. For instance, you might ask "When R U free?" and when he answers, you send back "So when do you charge? LOL". Cute, but if he doesn't get it, you're going to send a lot more messages trying to explain yourself.

Emoticons can help clue him in to your state of mind. Say you just watched him batter his body playing a game of footy, you could suggest giving him a massage and add a winking face to show you want to make him feel better in other ways too. But the same rule for abbreviations applies here – don't go overboard. Here are the five top emoticons and when to use them.

The smile :-) or :)
can get you out of trouble if
you say something that can be
interpreted the wrong way.

The wink ;-) or ;)
adds a flirty nudge,
nudge to your text.

The blush :">
is ideal for showing you're
not a shameless vamping
vixen when you say
something a bit risqué.

The heart <3
is useful for helping you walk
that thin line between "Just
flirting with you" and "I really
have feelings for you".

The kiss :-* or x
works like the heart. Don't think
of it as a long romantic smooch;
it's more like a quick peck.

!#@*?

Punctuation does count when you text. Here's how to end your message.

!   **The exclamation mark** is the most valuable punctuation mark you have in your armoury. It instantly sets a light flirtatious tone that says, "Well, helloooo!", however, it can also be the most dangerous. Because when you start overusing it, you come off as needy and unconfident. To use properly, exclaim only once per text!

;   **The semicolon** is good for making a wink but may not be used in any other situation unless you are an English teacher.

.   **Full stop (period).** Since proper punctuation isn't really necessary with texting – and it's sexier to let your thoughts dangle – a stop is used only to say you don't want to continue the conversation.

? **The question mark** is friendly.
Any more screams impatience.

' **Apostrophes** are the equivalent of
texting spleen – completely unnecessary.

* **Asterisks** can substitute for words
you're too shy to write: Let's f*ck.

... **Dot, dot, dot** (aka ellipses) can be
used for passive-aggressive messages.
For example, "We could meet there...
or at my house" practically screams that
you want to meet at your house (without
actually having to say it). You can also
use ellipses to add a steamy undertone:
"Lying in bed... thinking of you... with
nothing on..."

RULE

Proofread words and numbers.

There is a world of difference in writing "Like you!" and "Lick you!", especially if you accidentally send the text to your boss instead of your boy.

RULE

Get your timing right.

When he replies to your text, don't instant-message him back; you're not a doctor on call. On the other hand, if you're having a flirt back-and-forth, don't wait too long either, or you'll lose the momentum. Ten minutes is a good balance between the two.

Bad Connection: Never send a text at 3am asking if they're awake.

7

RULE

Be the first to hang up.

Texting is a quick tease, not an all-day affair. You don't want to bore him. So after a short chat, say you have to go and you'll text him later, then wait a day before picking up where you left off.

Ice Breakers

You spot him across a crowded room.

There is eye contact. Your heart beats a little faster, palms are sweaty, you're light-headed and your suddenly squeamish stomach has dropped to your knees. You're either suffering from an onset of food poisoning or you're in love. Unfortunately, unless you know someone who knows him, you're still going to have to approach him the old-fashioned way to get his number. If asking straight out is not your style, here are nine sneaky ways to get in touch with him so you can start flirxting.

📱 Give him your phone number. When he calls, his number will show up on your caller ID.

Bad Connection: He may be using someone else's phone, so before sending any titillating texts, check to make sure the number is his.

📱 Look online for it. There are people-search sites (type "find cell phone" into your favourite search engine) where you can enter a person's name and get their digits – just make sure you specify that you're looking for a mobile phone number.

📱 Tell him you're trying to break the *Guinness Book of World Records* for the most friends on a social network and ask him to friend you. Lots of people put their mobile phone on their profile.

📱 Tell him you can't find your phone and can he call your number so you can figure out where it is. His number will show up on your call log.

📱 In the middle of chatting to him, look at your watch and say you have to go, but you really want to finish the conversation so can you have his number to call him.

📱 Ask if he knows a good mechanic – guys always love giving car advice. When he starts to give you the info, say you have the memory of a gnat and you'd rather call him to get it.

📱 Learn a magic trick: hand him a small notepad and ballpoint pen (felt-tip won't work) and ask them to write down his phone number, making sure you can't see it, then tell him to destroy the paper however he wants. You will now make his number appear by virtue of your amazing witchy powers. Take a pencil and lightly rub against the next page on the notepad. The numbers he wrote should appear as a result of the impression made from the ballpoint. Abracadabra!

📱 Try calling a number from your phone and then make like your phone has run out of power. Ask if you can borrow his and call your own number.

📱 Get cute and say you lost your number so can you have his?

Once you have his number, go ahead and text him.

But keep it short and sweet. Most phones can't handle more than 160 characters anyway, and end up breaking the message into two texts or, worse, cutting you off before you're finished so you could end up sending "R U hot and bothered" when you really meant to say, "R U hot and bothered by the lame music in this club?" Try one of these if your brain crashes after typing "Hey!".

📱 For a no-risk first contact, just send a blank text. He'll probably reply asking if you were trying to text him. You can write you didn't know you had texted him, but ask "Wassup" or, if you want to get cute, write "My phone must be missing you".

📱 A good conversation starter is to send, "It's 11.11 – time 2 make a wish!" (This can be sent any time of the day when the hour and minutes are the same: 10.10, 5.55, 3.33...) Follow up in 15 minutes and ask him what he wished for. A good close: "I hope ur wish comes true!"

📱 To find out quickly if he is interested without too much risk, send, "My name is (insert name here) but u can call me 2night!" He'll call back within the hour if he wants more than a casual connection.

📱 Multitask your full-frontal flirt by sending him a text while you're still having your initial meet-up with these oh-so-frisky lines: "Who is that amazing woman you're talking to?" or "What if I said 'I like you' — would you text back and say you like me?"

📱 Jumpstart some immediate intimacy by referring to something that happened when you first met him, such as "Think that guy ever got his drink?"

Bad Connection: You run out of dialogue mid-text. It happens. You don't know this guy well enough to have a long, deep conversation — and that's not what texting is for anyway. It's for getting you to the point where you have a date so you can have those long, deep, 160+ character conversations. So if you run out of words, just say you have to go but you'll talk later (see Rule 7 on page 17). Leaving him hanging in this way will keep him wanting more.

📱 Think of
your texts as the same
conversation you might have
if you just met him. So at this early
stage of the game, don't type anything
you wouldn't speak out to his face. Just
because it's easier to type something
like "Hey, you big boy, show me what ur
packin'" than say it, that doesn't mean
you should. If you're unsure, try mirroring
his tone and style. If he uses a lot of
texting shorthand like "ur" for "you
are" you can follow suit. If he
uses proper English, do
likewise.

Bad connection: "How was ur weekend?" It's hard to get flirty if you ask him questions that he can answer in one word, so put him on the hook by staying open-ended. Here are some good texts for sending about two hours after you first meet:

"Stop talking about me to ur friends... what r you saying?"

"Miss me yet?"

"Staying out of trouble today?" *

"Hey, I got to thinking about you today..." *

(* He may give a one-word answer, but these questions are coquettish enough to let you ask a follow-up without sounding like you're interrogating him.)

R U D8ING?

Texting makes dating a lot easier, but you cannot date by text alone.

Getting to First Date

You've flirxted your way to making your first date. It probably seems easier to text with an offer to meet up, but it's also easier for him to type "No" and leave you hanging, wondering why. Also, research has shown that asking for things "in real time" makes it more likely for the intended to say "Yes". So, if he's not sure about it or he doesn't want to hurt your feelings, it's easy to decline or ignore your text request. Ask him in person or over the phone, and it's harder for him to turn you down. Plus, there's something so informally booty-callish about texting a request for a first date.

However, should you call and he replies, "Sure, text me", follow up immediately with, "I'm texting – when and where?" If he doesn't respond within ten minutes, delete his digits from your contact list. To get that first date by texting, not calling, here are a few ideas.

* If you'd really rather text than make that first call, then now is the time to be specific:

"Wanna meet (name a specific day and time)?" You can add an emoticon to take the directness out of it.

* If you want to pussyfoot up to the subject, then type:

"Will you go out with me pleeeeaaaasssseee?"

* Unlike asking on the phone, when you would want to make your plans in advance, keep it looser:

"R U up for a coffee later today?"

Bad Connection: Don't skip calling each other completely. If all you do is text, you don't have a relationship – you have a mobile chat room.

On the day of your date, put your phone on hold. Continuous texting hours before you meet can leave you speechless when you finally get together. It can be hard enough making conversation when your relationship is still wet behind the ears, let alone after you've already exchanged the details of your past 24 hours. These are the only three acceptable texts:

"Looking forward to 2night"

"Where and/or what time are we meeting"

"I will be wearing a burka" (or some other identifying wardrobe item)

The Follow-Up Date

The second date is actually much more crucial than the first one. After all, you had an electronic flirtation going on, then you probably had a casual meeting where you had a lot to say because you were getting up close and personal for the first time, but now your text chat is going to get a lot more intense.

First Question: **When Can You Text?**

In pre-text days, the unofficial rule was to wait three days before calling. Seventy-two hours of waiting, wondering, going wacky. But with SMS, the game has changed. Generally, the same day or night after your date is fine. You can wait 24 hours — but that's it. Any longer and you're saying you don't want to hear from him. He has (hopefully) taken the initiative and texted you by now, anyway.

You don't have to get sexy or coy or even ask about getting together again. Here are the top post-first-date texts and when to use them.

Within 24 hours of your tête à tête:

"I had a great time and wanted you to know"

"Should we replay?"

"I just heard someone with the same snort laugh as that man we sat next to – except his sounded even more like a pig's!"

"I sooo know ur thinking about me"

"Stop!" (He'll probably reply "Stop what?")
You reply: "Stop thinking about me. See, you're doing it... right... now..."

Within three days, send a general "keep me in your thoughts" text:

"My fish Goldie just did the funniest thing..."

"Did you see (name popular TV show) – what is up with (name most controversial character or plot line)."

Once you have set up your next date, you can send him a hot-under-the-collar note:

"I wish you were – sigh – here"

"I had the sexiest dream last night and you were in it!"

Bad Connection: Writing "I had a great time tonight… did you?" is fine until the last two words, which morph the whole text into a needy "Do you really like me?" cry. Also, because it can be answered with a simple yes or (worse) no, it's not going to get you very far. Much better would be a comment on something you did such as, "Loved the food/plot/venue but what was with the dog-faced waitress/weird ending/dishwater lattes? Next time you pick the restaurant/movie/café."

Once he texts back, you can get more up close and personal. If you don't hear from him after three texts, see Rule 1 of texting on page 9. Bottom line: he has dozens of ways to get in touch with you – texting, IMing, Facebook, tweeting, phoning. So don't make any excuses for a guy who doesn't connect.

Decode This Text

Read between his lines.

"Hey, what's up"
With no question mark, there's no reply needed. Good news — he's thinking of you but doesn't want to seem clingy or demanding.

"What R U up 2?"
When sent during daylight hours he actually does want to know. Don't text back a novel, just say you're kind of busy but hoping to have some downtime later. This gives you an out in case he is just enquiring casually, but also lets him know you are free if he wants to get together.

"What R U up 2?"
If sent early evening, he's bored and didn't make plans. Get together if you want to; he may just be bad at organizing his life.

"What R U up 2?"
If sent after 10 pm, he's horny.
Lady's choice.

"I Love You"
If sent before midnight he's actually saying,
"I just realized how incredibly lucky I am to
have you in my life, but am too shy to tell
you face to face."

"I Love U"
If sent after midnight it means: I'm drunk,
I'm lonely and feeling sorry for myself and
you feel better than my right hand.

**"What are you up to tonite ...
wanna go out?"**
Do you really need to decode this one?

"NO JLY LVE B#^ – OK?"
He's so geeky he speaks in code
or he's drunk.

"You had me at hello" or any line from a movie

He wants to let you know he's interested, but is not sure what to say.

He answers "Maybe" when you ask if he wants to get together

He may really not be sure when he is free or he may be unable to commit to even a time. Ask him straight out when he will he sure.

He keeps texting and texting and texting

Did you notice his sore thumb when you went out? He's just showing you he's into you. If you don't mind his play-by-play, all is good. If it's getting borderline weird, ask him to turn off his phone for a bit.

Umm...

Fine in conversation but if he is going to the effort to write it down, it means he isn't comfortable with whatever you just wrote and he's hoping you'll take the hint.

You're a Couple

Once you're established, it's easy to slip into bad texting where you're just giving each other quick updates like "I'm running late". But the longer you're together, the more crucial it is to stay intimate.

> This is when texts really come into their own. If you stay lovingly in touch throughout the day, it's much easier to get physically in touch once you're together. This isn't about getting raunchy (that comes later!); it's about wooing each other with words to strengthen your bond.
>
> Tell him how good he smells or that you were having a down day until you remembered the morning kiss he gave you; or try random sweet talk like:
>
> "What would we be doing if I was there with you right now?"
>
> "U + ME = 4EVER"

SECTION TWO

I WANT YOUR TEXT

Words have tremendous power, so it doesn't take much to transform your text from an instant info source into heat-seeking missiles ("I'm at the grocery … picking up a can of whipped cream for later"). A "sext" message is discreet, quick and can most definitely be dirty. Even the simplest phrases like "I'm about to take a bath" can conjure up powerful fantasies.

There are loads of ways to get sexting. You can surprise-send your partner with an out-of-the-blue "Hey stud, thinking of you" message to jumpstart passion or get naughty and text some squirm-worthy "hot for you" line when on your way to your date. You can even send a triple X, like "I forgot to put on underwear", when you're already together in a crowded place to add a thrilling tint to your time together. Think of it as getting bonus time for foreplay. Whichever way, you'll definitely set the scene for a hot night.

Getting Sexting

While this sort of texting may make you feel tongue-tied, it definitely comes with benefits (wink, wink). When you've been doing the same old, same old with the same old, a spicy sext can fire up a stale love life. Even if you're in a long-distance relationship, you can still work each other into a frenzy. If you're on the shyer side, texting can be an under-the-table way to let your man know what you like (and don't like) sexually or a way to explore your wild side. Another plus: it's safe (no chance of STIs or unwanted pregnancy) and cheap (that imaginary lingerie and other tools of seduction don't cost a thing).

The hardest part is getting started, so here's a few guidelines before you get sexty.

📱 Instead of getting hung up trying to sound like a porn star or come up with some erotic fantasy, just tell him what you're thinking or feeling. The key? KISS (Keep it simple, sweetheart). You don't have to send long, involved sex plots – your message can simply be: "SEXSEXSEXSEXSEXSEXSEX".

📱 Have a sense of what's sexy for both of you – how explicit do you want to get? He's going to mirror his responses to your language, so think about what words turn you on. A good rule of thumb is to use text messaging to set the mood for the kind of sex you want to have, be it sweet, gentle lovemaking, animal passion or whatever else floats your boat.

📱 Abbreviations and emoticons are not sexy. Spell out the full word.

📱 If you're not sure about the tip above, read a romance novel to see how they do it. Don't worry if it sounds cheesy. All dirty talk is cheesy!

📱 Pet names, writing "Hey sexy" or "Hi handsome", are all to be encouraged.

📱 Mix up your raunch with romance. Instead of always writing a play-by-play of your sex life, occasionally throw in a simple "I love you" or any variation such as "I adore you/j'taime/ you rock my world/you are my world".

📱 If he asks what you're wearing, don't say an old Blur T-shirt with holes in it. Lie and tell him you have on pasties and a thong – the more detailed you get, the better.

📱 Sexting is definitely a great way to dip your toe in and see if your partner is up for experimenting, but build up to your secret desire. Unless you're texting that you want him to watch you make out with another girl, he may feel uncomfortable trying something new (and may take it as a blow to his stud abilities). One little trick is to first get him hot under the collar with some standard sexy texts. He's more likely to try something new if he's already steamed up.

Bad Connection: He wants to do what?!? Not everything he texts will be something you're totally up for. If you don't know how to respond, play for time with an "mmmm" or a few kisses and hugs or, if you want to throw cold water on his suggestion, a "LOL". If he freaks over something you text, LOL also works as a face-saver to pretend you were just goofing around.

Go ahead and send him a series of messages, building up what you would like to do to him in each one. Keep it quick, direct and to the point.

43

Bad Connection: Don't expect instant gratification when you send him a sexy text. He may be unable to respond right away or he may be figuring out how to respond in kind. If you want to make sure he is available for some teasing texts, start by asking if he's free to play. Or concoct a code to let him know you're about to send some erotic inspirations by saying you're sending coming attractions. This way he'll know not to check his texts if it's not a convenient time.

Know
when not to text.
This should go without
saying, but do not text
during sex – even each other.
Nothing kills the mood more like
the loud and abrupt buzzing of an
incoming text when you're in bed.
To avoid any unwanted textual
interruptions, turn off your
phones. Whatever it is,
it can wait.

Sext Me Up

Now for some no-sweat ways to heat up your texts.

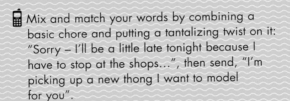 Mix and match your words by combining a basic chore and putting a tantalizing twist on it: "Sorry – I'll be a little late tonight because I have to stop at the shops...", then send, "I'm picking up a new thong I want to model for you".

Double whammy by sending him a seemingly innocent text and then following up right away with a sexy finish: "I like those jeans you had on last night...", then send, "All I could think about was taking you home and taking them off".

Tell him what it is about him that turns you on. Picture his body, the way he moves, the way he touches you, then describe it: "I love running my fingers over your pecs, down your six-pack and straight to your hard package".

📱 Or focus on something he does to you: "I was in the shower soaping myself getting hot thinking about the way you stroke my lips" – leave him guessing which lips!

📱 Add a sexy slant to his texts. For instance, if he messages, "I'm going to sleep now", text back right away, "You're in bed? Mmmm".

📱 If everything you write sounds cheesy, stick with the five senses; let him know how you're yearning for his touch, or how you want to feel his skin against yours. Describe caresses, moans, hot breath, salty skin and so on.

📱 All-purpose sexy text: compliment his body, bodacious bawdy abilities or size.

The Three Rs

Writer's block? Get him hot and bothered in 15 words or less with these pleasure-pitching texts. Choose your mood.

Romantic

These little love notes will put you in his mind and in his heart.

"I want to feel your eyes on my body, your breath on my face..."

"Your smile makes me melt"
"I dreamt of us last night"

"For the last 24 hrs, 1440 minutes, 86400 seconds, I've missed you"

"I love the feel, taste, touch, scent, sound of you"

"Did you dream of me last night?"

"I love the way you make me feel"

"I'm in the mood for you"

"Thinking about you right now"

"Close your eyes and imagine I'm kissing you right this second"

"You take my breath away"

"Kisses, Kisses, Kisses"

"You make my head – and body – melt"

"I need you tonight"

"XXXXXXXXXXXXXXXXXXXX"

Racy

Send one of these frisky texts and it may
be all the foreplay you need.

> "What are you wearing?"
>
> "Text dirty to me"
>
> "Want to play later?"
>
> "I wish you were lying next to me"
>
> "I can almost feel you touching me...
> caressing me... loving me..."
>
> "I can't wait to feel your touch all
> over my body"
>
> "I want to make love to you every minute
> of every day"
>
> "I want to get naked with you right now"

"I got a new showerhead – the detachable kind. The pressure's awesome"

"Don't work out too much… save your energy for later"

"I just picked up some chocolate sauce – do you want to be dessert?"

"Picture me naked"

"I'm planning on giving you a good rubdown later"

"You look so hot in those jeans"

"Tell me what you would do to me if we were naked"

"I have a pair of lacy red panties on… they feel so soft to the touch"

"You sexy beast"

Bad Connection: It will kill the mood if he has to guess at your meaning – a booty text needs to be quick and dirty.

Be Bold Use explicit direct adjectives (a thesaurus can come in handy) to stoke him. So instead of a simple line like "I love the way you kiss me", try "I love your soft kisses on my neck. It makes me wet!"

Be Blunt No beating around the bush. Call body parts as you see them. Instead of just texting "I love your body", try "I love the feel of your hard, meaty cock when you're thrusting into me".

Be Bad This isn't about playing hard to get, it's about making him hard.

Raunchy

These libido-lifting lines are guaranteed
to get a rise out of him.

"I love that crazy thing you do with
your tongue"

"I need a spanking tonight. I've been very,
very bad..."

"I love the way you suck me... I want
you to do it all night..."

"You're so hot and sexy!"

"Can't wait to get you naked tonight"

"You make me so horny"

"I can see your bulge in your jeans.
Mmmm. Sexy"

"Think of me as your slave tonight… your wish is my command"

"I want to feel your hot, wet lips all over me"

"Join me in the tub tonight for some steamy sex"

"Are you getting all hot and bothered thinking about my body?"

"I want to touch you here… and here… and there…"

"Tonight I want you to just lie back and let me ravage you"

"Sex me up, baby"

"I want to run my hands all over your hard chest"

Bad Connection: You texted, you sexted and now you never want to see him again. You could take the indirect approach and "acci-text" him: you send a text bad-mouthing him to him but address it as if you are sending it to your inner circle.

However, if you do want a redial on your connection, then send him one of these the morning after:

"Stud!"

"I loved that thing you did to me last night"

"I can still smell you on my skin. Sweet"

Sexty Mad Libs: Fill in the Blank

"It makes me [adjective] when I think about you touching my [noun]."

"I want you to [verb] me"

"I'm wearing [noun]"

"I'm not wearing [noun]!"

"Want to know what I'd do if you were here [verb]?"

"Hey babe. I just got out of the shower and started rubbing [noun] all over me"

"Can you touch your [noun] right now for me and tell me how it feels?"

"I love when you [verb] me"

Bad Connection: Long-distance sexting is the perfect way to keep the carnal communication going when you're apart, but it will lose its raunchy appeal if it's all talk and no action; up the erotic ante by simultaneously masturbating. Explain to each other exactly what you're doing – "I'm tracing circles on my breasts" – and how it's feeling – "I'm getting so wet". It's easier to give "good phone" if you get in a lusty mood, so stoke up with some pre-strokes before dialing his digits.

SECTION THREE

DIRTY TALK

Even if you're not blessed with a throaty voice, a sailor's vocabulary and the confidence to get hot and heavy over the phone, you can master the art of aural sex. If the thought of making a dirty call leaves you speechless, here's your by-the-numbers phone plan for making a carnal connection.

1 When to call?

Definitely when you are apart for any length of time. Think about it – he is going to be a lot less tempted by any nearby babes if he has a hot phone date with you. And reconnecting physically will be easier if you have stayed – nudge, nudge – intimately in touch via the phone.

Never call before lunch. Timing is everything. Call him when the day has just begun and instead of concentrating on your sexy soliloquies, he'll be checking emails, sorting through paperwork and organizing his day. By midday, he will be more in the mood to take a (heavy) breather.

Giving good phone is a lot easier – and more fun – if you get into a lusty mood before you dial. Lie back and envision a supercharged bedroom scenario with your guy. Start stroking yourself, and when your pulse is pounding, give him a call.

2 Where to call?

Find a place where you can talk – or do other things, wink wink – in privacy. It could be the bedroom, the bathtub or, if you're at work, a quiet room where you won't be unexpectedly disturbed.

Create a steamy mood to put yourself in the right mindset. Have a playlist of tunes that turn you on, read some raunchy fiction or daydream about your sexiest encounter (you may want to reel in these props to help you get your conversational mojo on once the two of you are chatting).

Lower or turn off the lights (fluorescent is not conducive to any erotic encounter – ever).

3 Sex up your voice.

Tone is everything. You could be reading the encyclopedia and make it sound like you're in nooky nirvana. Or you could say the dirtiest thing in the world and make it sound like the voice on the GPS. The easiest way to sound off is to whisper in a low voice. Think breathy and husky, like you just smoked a 20-pack.

Slow it down. Don't go at your usual 100 words-per-minute pace. Make it long and drawn out. He will be hanging on your every "um" and "er".

Remember to breathe. Draw those exhales out to avoid sounding like you're in the gym working out.

Smile, no matter what. When you smile, you sound enthusiastic, even if your face is redder than a baboon's bum.

Show some enthusiasm. You're not being forced at gunpoint here. He wants to feel that you're enjoying the moment as much as he is.

4 Talk dirty to him, baby!

It's time to say something. The key is to keep it simple at first. Saying "I miss you" in the right tone can be enough for him to hear "I miss you in my bed, loving me, touching me, making me whimper".

Emphasize certain words to up your amorous antics: "What do you want to do *now*?", "I wish you were here with me, *right now*", "I *love* when you say my name." Or speak in code – "Tease me" or "Let's do my favourite thing" – things that only you two know, making it seem like you have your own private dirty language. You don't need to use dirty language to speak dirty.

Run out of things to say? Praise his body. Tell him what you're going to do to him when you're together. Or get yourself off the hook by asking him what he wants to do to you. If he gets tongue-tied, have a naughty magazine or book to hand so you can read out steamy sections.

Get graphic. Skip the poetry or getting fancy. You don't have to wow him with your lusty linguistics. Have you ever heard amazing porn movie dialogue? Exactly. All he wants is to hear how big and hard you think he is, how much you want him and how good he makes you feel. You can simply narrate your action: "I am touching my breasts, Oh! my nipples are so hard for you, I am touching myself between my legs, Oh! I am getting so wet for you" and so on.

5

Don't forget to talk back.

He wants to know you are responding to what he is saying. You can murmur, "Mmmm, mmmm," throw in a few "ooohs" and "ahhhs" or simply breathe heavy. To really make his ears burn, pretend you're having a big O – or maybe you don't need to pretend? Go for it, girl!

6 Don't be afraid to lie.

If he asks you what you are doing and you're multitasking washing the dishes while dirty talking, say you're in the bath. If he asks what you're wearing and you're in your favourite flannel PJs, tell him you have on sexy lingerie. If he asks where you are and you're hiding in the ladies' at work, tell him you're naked in a fitting room at Agent Provocateur. The more detailed you get, the better, because it makes it easier for him to envision you in all of your sexy glory.

7 Spill your secret vices.

Just because you're saying something doesn't mean it has to happen when you're together. The more you can fire up his imagination – and yours – the more frisky fun you will have. If he responds with a horrified silence to something you say, a quick facesaver to lighten things up is to give a little giggle and switch back to a fantasy you have heard him mention. He'll have forgotten about it in a flash.

8 **He wants you to do what?**

Never freak! This is fantasy speak – not the real thing. If he takes you by surprise, try not to speak as you will probably end up sounding shocked or disgusted. Instead, just give a quick "Mmm, mmmm" and, if you're really uncomfortable with the turn things are taking, take his mind off the subject by saying how hot you are. It will refocus his mind wonderfully.

9

Work your digits.

Remember, aural sex isn't all talk and no action. Up the X factor by simultaneously masturbating. Explain to each other exactly what you're doing ("I'm tracing circles inside my thighs") and how it's feeling ("I'm getting so hot").

10

Hang it up.

The hardest part of a dirty phone conversation is actually ending it. Make sure he's done first, so don't stop him mid-sentence. You can simply say "I love you", "I miss you" or "I can't wait to see you". Or, if you want to leave him squirming, try something like "Bye, I'm going bed now and imagine my hands are yours…"

PICTURE IT

Humans — and particularly men — are visual creatures. So one jpeg can say 1,000 LHSXs. Getting or sending a sexy snap always feels playful and naughty at the same time, and doing it is as easy as taking your clothes off. But before you suck in your belly, twist your torso oh-so-artfully and stick that booty out, think: that picture you're about to send is a permanent file; a file that can be emailed, posted or re-texted.

So sending a sexy picture is essentially stating "I trust you completely". If that's not something you'd say to him while staring deeply into his eyes, then hold off on the photo shoot. And if you haven't trusted your vagina to him yet, it's probably best not to trust a picture of your vagina to him either. Keep him interested the old-fashioned way, with slow, meaningful texts.

Even if you've been together forever, you should still hold something back when sending a picture. He might accidentally leave his phone out and viewable when with his mates or inadvertently flip it open during a business meeting.

Sexy Snaps

There are loads of ways to upload your image without compromising yourself. Here's how to give him your best shot.

📷 You in a full bubble bath with the message "I'm all wet for you".

📷 Slip into a sexy negligée in bed and send with the message "Later?".

📷 A close-up of your fingers or shoulder with the question: "Guess what this is!".

📷 A picture of just your lips forming a kiss.

📷 You in any outfit that shows off your curves: a bikini, a clingy dress, a scarf that covers all the right places. Add the text, "You can unwrap me tonight".

📷 Do something sexy like lick a lollipop, squirt whipped cream into your mouth or simply suck your finger.

- 📷 Take a picture of you blowing him a kiss.

- 📷 If you know he has a secret fantasy like seeing you dressed up as a nurse or schoolteacher, get into costume and zap it to him with a wink.

- 📷 Send a series of teasing snaps working from the top of your body down: your eyes, your lips, the curve of your neck, your shoulder, a glimpse of cleavage, your belly button, your hips, your just pedi'd foot...

- 📷 Turn the above into a slow striptease, but never send anything explicit – show yourself slowly removing a long glove or unpinning your hair or removing your bra from the back.

- 📷 Photoshop your head onto a famous body – and add a joke to make the home-editing job obvious, such as "Your Frankenstein lover".

- 📷 Play sext poker – it's like strip poker except you do it through texts and photos. Take turns sending picture messages of yourselves gradually taking off your clothes without showing anything explicit.

Bad Connection: If you can't help yourself, try unique shots that don't show your face or any identifying marks. Or next time you want to get naughty and naked, try Skyping each other (there's no dangere of a permanent record!).

Dos and Don'ts

It's crazy-easy to amp up the voltage on your wireless connection by sending a naughty photo, but the world is full of horny repressed geeks with the technological skill to access your system and steal anything you send online. Before you take it all off, know your dos from your don'ts.

Do know the laws of sending sexy pics in your neck of the woods.

Don't ever send a pic if either of you are under age or if a minor has access to the pic.

Do ensure your background area looks inviting.

Don't slip into your birthday suit if you plan on running for political office, if he's any kind of webmaster or you just met him in a chatroom.

Do remember that screens are really small so close-ups of body parts like belly buttons or a shoulder are much sexier than a full-body money shot.

Don't ever let him think that receiving a close-up his little monster is a turn on.

SECTION FIVE

BAD TEXT

Texting comes with its own set of rules and etiquette. Read on for texts you shouldn't send and toxic texters.

Step Away From the Phone

When you...

Are under the influence.

Chances are you were too blotto to make sense anyway. But if you told that cute guy that you met just yesterday that you want to have his children, the best damage control is silence. If he does ask what's up, pretend that whatever you wrote is an old joke you meant to text to your best friend.

Are pissed off.

Once it's in writing, it's harder to take back. Also, because emotion is so easily misread via text, you can end up being misunderstood, resulting in worse fights that last longer than if you had been face to face. Anyway, it doesn't matter how succinct you are, you need more than 160 characters to sort things out. So if you do angry text, follow up ASAP with a "We need to talk" call. You can apologize, but you still need to get together soon — for the makeup sex if nothing else.

Can't think of anything to say.

If you text-spam him, he'll be less likely to focus on your words when you actually have something important to say.

Want to say "I love you" for the first time.

Honestly, you can't really think that is OK!

Want to break up.

When giving someone the heave-ho, at least extend him the courtesy of a phone call.

Are driving.

Two words – car crash. If you insist, at least get good insurance.

Are out with someone.

Rude, rude, rude. If you must, lie and say your cat is at the vet and you were checking on her.

Discover you did not delete your ex's phone number.

Post-breakup 3 am "What R U doin?" texts are almost always followed by late-night romps and early morning regrets. If you must "ex text", at least block his replies.

Just texted him two seconds before.

You can check if you sent the text to the right number, so you don't need to desperate dial and ask if he got it. If you must text, at least redirect it to a friend who can talk you back to sanity.

Just texted someone whom you would not want to accidentally receive a sexy message from you.

It's too easy to make a mistake and send your love note to the wrong person. Triple check those digits before pressing "Send".

Toxic Texters

Nine texters you should hang up on.

Serial Texter

Yes, texting is easy but
relationships are not, and you
need to know he has what it takes
to be in one with you. If he's too busy
to call, he's too busy to be in love.
One way to get him to dial your
number is to send a text saying,
"Unlike your carrier, I don't offer
unlimited texting – call me
tonight!"

Tight-Lipped Texter

He keeps it so short and to the point, you don't have a clue what he's saying. Just keep texting "?" back until he gets it.

Touch-Base Texter

He texts some variation of "Hello" throughout the day. Fine one time, but after a while he begins to sound like a lonely echo. Reply with a specific question, "What R U doing?" "Meet up l8ter?", "How's work?" None will turn him into a blabbermouth, but at least you have a clearer idea of his day.

Mass Texter

He sends the same email to every woman he knows. Mass text everyone he knows, saying he's a loser.

Texty-Feely

He bombards you with love messages all day long. After a while you begin to feel smothered, so think carefully about whether this is a habit you really want him to break. If so, ignore him. It may take a while, but he'll slow down.

Public Texter

There is no excuse for sharing anything you sent him privately. He doesn't respect you. Public text break-up with him.

No Texter

Is he ignoring you or is it that he just doesn't like to text? If it's the latter, no biggie, as long as he calls. If it's the former, he's telling you that you're not important to him.

The Untimely Texter

There is such a thing as too late or too early to text. Unless one of you is a werewolf or an early bird, texts before 8 am and after midnight are unacceptable. This is what email is for.

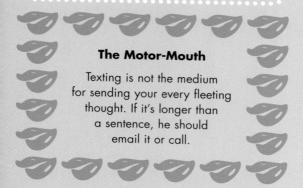

The Motor-Mouth

Texting is not the medium for sending your every fleeting thought. If it's longer than a sentence, he should email it or call.

SECTION SIX

LET'S HAVE TEXT

The problem with texting is that you only have so many words and characters to say everything you want to say. Use the "textionary" on the following pages to learn how to work your keys.

If You Want to Say...   Press...

A

If You Want to Say...	Press...
Age/Sex/Location (availability)	ASL, A/S/L/A
All my love	AML
Anytime, anywhere, anyplace	A3
Are you single?	RUS
As a friend	AAF
At the end of the day	@TEOTD

B

If You Want to Say...	Press...
Big crush on/Big crush on you	BCO/BCOY
Big grin/Big evil grin	BG/BEG
Big tease	TT
Booty call	BTYCL
Boyfriend	BF, BOYF
Bye for now	B4N

C

If You Want to Say...	Press...
Call me	CM
Check your email	CYE
Chuckle, snicker, grin	CSG
Cool	KEWL
Crying	):
Cutie, Cutie pie	QT, QUTI

D

Deep wet passionate kiss on the lips	DWPKOTL
Don't sweat it	DSI
Down for sex?	D46?
Do you have a boyfriend/girlfriend?	DYHAB/G
Do you scream out loud?	DUSL

E

Exciting	X-1-10

F

Face to face	F2F
Faster	XLR8
Forever and ever	4EAE

G

Get your pants off	GYPO
Girlfriend	GF, GRLF
Got a picture?	GAP
Great big hug	GBH

H

Hate	8
Have a good night	HAGN
Have fun	HF
Hmmm? or What did you say?	:S

Hope to see you soon	H2CUS
Hot for you	H4Y
How about you?	HBU
Hug, Hugs	H,O
Hugs and kisses	O&K, 88,
	H&K, HAK
Hug back	HB

I

I could fall in love with you	ICFILWU
I don't know	404
I hate you	182
I like you	IYQ
I love you	143/459/ILU/
	ILY
I'm busy	IMBZ
I miss you	IMU
Intense text sex	ITS
It's over	86
I want sex now	IWSN
I will always love you	IWALU

J

Jacking off	J/O

K

Kiss	X
Kiss(es) for you	K4Y /KFY/
	KFU
Kiss, hug, kiss, hug	XOXO
Kiss, kiss	KK
Kiss on lips (cheek)	KOL/KOC
Kiss with serious tongue action	KWSTA
Kissy-sound	MUAH/
	MWAH

L

Later	L8R
Laugh out loud/lots of laughs/ lots of love	LOL
Left voicemail	LVM
Let's fuck	LF
Let's have sex	LH6/LHSX
Let's meet in real life	LMIRL
Like to go?/(I'd) love to go	L2G
Long-distance relationship	LDR
Lots of love	LOL, LOLO
Love you	LY
Love you so much	LUSM/LYSM

M

Miss you (so much)	MU/MUSM
My true love, always	MTLA

N

Naked in front of computer	NIFOC

P

Please call me	PCM
Please explain that	PXT

R

Reply not necessary	RNN

S

Sealed with a kiss	SWAK
See you in my dreams	CUIMD
See you/See you too	CU/CU2
Sexy	6Y
Sideways heart	<3 (more 3s mean a bigger heart)
Smile/Big smile	*s*, :) /:D
Someone with me	SOWM

T

Talk dirty to me	TDTM
Talk to you later	TTUL/TTYL/
	TLK2UL8R
Text me back (later)	TMB/TBL
Thanks	10X
That's all for now	TAFN
Thinking about you, miss you,	
always love you	TAUMUALU
Tomorrow	2MOR
Tomorrow evening	TPM
Tonight	2NTE
Too good to be true	2G2BT
Too much too handle	2M2H

W

Will you call me?	WYCM
Wink	*w*, ;)

Y

You're hot	URH
You're sexy	URS
You make my fingers sweat	YMMFS